DRAWING ON PREVIOUS LEARNING

MIKE FERGUSON

DRAWING ON PREVIOUS LEARNING
MIKE FERGUSON

All rights reserved. No part of this book may be reproduced, stored in a retrieval system or transmitted in any form or by any means electronic, mechanical, photocopying, recording or otherwise, without the prior permission of the publisher.

ISBN 978-1903110799

First published in this edition 2021 by Wrecking Ball Press.

Copyright: Mike Ferguson

Cover design: humandesign.co.uk

All rights reserved.

Mike Ferguson taught English for 30 years at an 11-18 comprehensive school in Devon, 18 as Head of Department, and he was also a Senior Examiner of GCSE English Literature for over 35 years.

His passion for teaching English was fully fostered in the first half of a career where a professional independence in the job was supported and encouraged, this always underpinned by the joy of working with students, especially creatively, and like-minded colleagues. The later years of external influences, built on the platforms of target setting and linked school measurements, did much to counter and interfere with the intuition for exploring and being creative in English as a subject.

His examining career followed a similar trajectory, the early years of this fully reflecting the spirit of students' engagement and independent responses. Although this spirit continues to be rewarded in the principles of assessment, the more recent years of a knowledge-based curriculum and again the pressures of targets and measurements have skewed some teaching and student responses away from this.

Acknowledgements

Some of the poems in Drawing On Previous Learning previously appeared in the following collections and online journals:

Nearing the Border – Stride
Precarious Real – Maquette Press
Professions – The Red Ceilings Press
International Times
Litbreak Magazine
Stride Magazine
The Writers' Café Magazine

CONTENT

Teacher	11
Art Teachers	13
Plum Tree Rain	14
Teacher Training	15
SPaG MCQs	16
Root Canal	17
Beliefs and Values Teachers	18
Crushed Stetson	19
In Media Res	20
English Teachers	21
Homework	22
Flattening the Grass	23
Geography Teachers	24
Who Killed the Thought-Fox	25
History Teachers	26
Lacking Lemov	27
Dynamic Learning	28
ICT Teachers	31
More and More	32
21st June	33
Prior Knowledge	36
Modern Languages Teachers	37
National Curriculum at Sea Life	38
Maths Teachers	39

Aeolian Harping On	40
Angel	42
Crooks	43
Prior Knowledge Encore	44
PE Teachers	45
Sausages	46
Creativities Passport	47
Learning Support Teachers	49
A Student is Singing	50
Pathetic Fallacy	51
Science Teachers	52
All Doom and Little Freedom	53
T F&D Teachers	54
Where Do Ex-Students Go?	55
A Bold Cold Autumn	57
Music and Drama Teachers	58
Mr Fergy	59
Debbie	61
Where Do Ex-Teachers Go?	62
Understood	64
Caesura	65
On My First Job	66
Students	67

TEACHER

Dressed in a dreary suit
with the laughter inside
barbed hours

what you say and do
is commando

is management

is dispensing remedies.

The multitudinous ways
you love
genuflects

the wire of hours,

manifests your pain
as ennui

as where it discovers

as curator to the snake.

Here is where
you discover
the meanings

of chore

of clerking

of the crawl.

All the most
memorable jokes
have sloughed.

ART TEACHERS

Art teachers who
know how colour is more than their words / use canvas when
paint is not enough / choose heliotrope for the tinge in painting
love / imagine through rainbow desire / paint sonnets in thirteen
colours / understand only metaphor explains and explores / think
surfing is sculpturing a wave / put curves in straight lines / are
happy to have two complete ears / believe that description is a
useless art / abhor black and white in education / use a palette
for being mixed-up / know Dali should design the curriculum /
brushstroke their lives

PLUM TREE RAIN

The plum tree is raining again – a light mist falling
from the leaves – so it is difficult to mark these
exam scripts. I have set up and moved to this table
to catch the early evening sun otherwise blocked by
tall conifers when I sit on the usual patio. Aphids
drip too, and there are wet spots where I swipe them
away as well as those finest drops that now mark the
dark wood though not on papers with their answers.
No doubt the writers in their intense over-training
will tell me it is a foreshadowing, a pathetic fallacy
about dampening down or a haze veiling meaning.
This is nonsense, but I can't explain how it is drizzling
without a cloud in the sky, not like specious coaches
or birds above pissing in laughter at their approaches.

TEACHER TRAINING

Teacher training
      for those who can
      leaning into the rails
      at one of the four
      with bells on
      without rhyme
      to the tune of Ray
      in four-part harmony
      unplanned
      whose art arcs science
      with the umbrella
      forever
      waiting for coffee
      with springs to leap woodcocks
      like foreplay
      for outer space
      spelt conceptually
      as a mirror
      before the heartbeat
      that knows its magic three
      in its paisley shirt
      playing the bongos
      riding the wave
      inside your head

SPaG MCQs

a. is this the way, you will ask? the question [or]
b. is this, the way, you will, ask the, question? [or]
c. Is this the way you will ask the question?

is this the way you will ask the question
this is the question the way you will ask
ask is this the way you question the will
is the way you will ask the question you
question is this the way you will the ask
will you ask is the question the you way
the question you ask is the way you will
is this the question the way you will ask

d. the question
   you will ask
   is this the way?

ROOT CANAL

Apart from one brief anticipation of pain
I am wonderfully numbed, the only
discomfort in the sustained large O I am
made to make whilst the drool and drilled
detritus is immediately and cleanly vacuumed
away. All I can do is count the exams I'd
have to mark to match the dentist's fee – and
going at a steady pace it's about three days.

Blood on the papers, screaming between the
lines, journeys to the roots of memory: rewarding
their pain is a channel to pleasures, one that
marked in red is like finding the large X to
signal where I have discovered treasures, their
route to a dentist's wage or teacher's imagination.

BELIEFS AND VALUES TEACHERS

Beliefs & Values teachers who
see the light as light / accept believing has its many voices / place palm to palm for the touch / understand that He is one of many myths / deplore what Sara did to Samuel / sing hymns in silence / mark homework on Sundays / genuflect with their thinking / understand a sonnet is the speech of fourteen different gods / know Luke was the insidious optimist / never confuse Santa with Satan on purpose / accept religion has its many vices / aren't waiting / also carry their own cross

CRUSHED STETSON

Doorways are portals to dreams, but when they close
cut like a guillotine. Red flows, and lust is layered on
the floor as a metaphor – and this cherry ink too
chastises or caresses. There is too much love of these
imaginings, how the combing of wet hair is an
ablution for the ridding of sins, or grooming for an
illicit affair. Someone is walking and talking but they are
really the litotes in a semantic field of verbs, now as
past participles of secret authorial meanings rather than
words. There are times when we need to see beyond that
single sketched line of the hill, see the other landscapes
that hide within the fog and fear, but eyes are for opening
not drawing on. In a room where someone is preaching,
better lessons are taught and learnt when chanced upon.

IN MEDIA RES

There's a sudden roll and roar
of percussion in media res on
Disc 6, which is Symphony No. 9
by Vaughan Williams, having
heard the 8th in D minor, this one
in E, the *Moderato maestoso*,
so just into the first movement,

yet it isn't and instead a plane
passing overhead with the window
opened at the desk where I listen,
marking students writing in Latin,
yet they don't and instead – like this
sound not in media res which would

be near the end of the 2nd, *Andante
sostenuto*, as if I understand
Italian – are playing with terms
like drum-thunder in a narrative
making noise flying above and so
unable to hear the real words below.

ENGLISH TEACHERS

English teachers who
career on a seasonal sledge / are as ambiguous as love / know
Godot will never / spell Santa with a sibilance of snow / listen to
meanings as they change / know an English emporium trades in
metaphor and error / will travel to nowhere they want to go / hear
Carver in the simplicity of everything unsaid / know a line can
rise and fall like now / fight philistinism for philosophical fun
/ write sonnets in the rhythm of sound / are aware when to let
themselves go / understand getting the chimney inside Santa / are
standing out on the edge

HOMEWORK

is school-work done at home homework
school-work done at home is homework
done school-work is homework at home
at home school-work is done homework
homework done at home is school-work
done homework is school-work at home
is homework done at home school-work
homework is school-work done at home

FLATTENING THE GRASS

They are not crafting elegant crop circles on the children. Assemblies of Humiliation even forget the good grace of gods. *Emphatic manner* is not quite water and towel, but it gets the torment done. It isn't the same as Lulu and the Luvvers singing *Shout*. Grass that grows will wave in the wind, this way and that, seemingly a thing of natural beauty. *Pretend interpretations* are just snowflakes falling in all weathers. In my day, there was an assembly reading of a Lawrence poem – *ugliness, ugliness* – and a student fell forward onto his face: it was a different kind of learning. Grouse moors and the e-cigarette industry burn and scorch in their own insidious ways.

GEOGRAPHY TEACHERS

Geography teachers who
would recognise a river from an airplane / have read Frank
Monkhouse / understand where Coleridge found god / give a care
about a spur / meander / love being physical / know a sonnet has
peaks and troughs / sense more about latitudes than storms / see
more about a shore / get it wrong and have a trip in a field / didn't
miss the gorge at Buxton / love the tease of an apex / promote
pantheism / see it all from the ground

WHO KILLED THE THOUGHT-FOX?

Perhaps it is the decline of winter
as a season - and I imagine now
the paw-prints at their best in a
layered snow - but it is more
than this: a cruel warmth
melts the habitat, and freedom to
roam has been curtailed by trips and
traps set by new hunters who know
no better. If this is acceptable
then anything else that could be
imagined to the full might as well
die too, and the murderers can come
running with their measuring tapes
sizing up this final kill.

HISTORY TEACHERS

History teachers who
know time tells what time hides / can explain the lineage
of royalty's reign / see beyond the storytelling / believe
Shakespeare's was before the Italian's / know statues stand to
fall when the narrative unravels / rewrite their own disasters as
success / remember when Labour was different to the Tories /
remember / accept that the future hasn't happened / understand
that music explains everything / extrapolate like gamblers / place
bets like clairvoyants / think their subject should teach lessons
/ can prove Ofsted was, is and always will be consigned / record
better times

LACKING LEMOV

1. Less is more: government initiatives should be limited to one side of A4
2. Targets are for archers, not teachers: adorn your classroom with who you are
3. League tables struggle to measure the sensitive inside leg
4. You can lead a horse to a test but that won't make it think for itself
5. Teaching is like riding a bike: when you fall off it hurts
6. Ofsted is awful: sound and symmetry and sense
7. If they're laughing they're learning
8. Don't wear a tie just to look like a teacher
9. A full house beats a flush and metaphor beats the literal, hands down
10. Praise *everything* said that is serious and genuine
11. The best objective is that which discovers itself by accident
12. Only one of the Gospels reports seeing a four-part lesson plan
13. The 'wrong' answer often reveals how learning works wonderfully
14. If a sonnet has 14 lines, is this a poem? Discuss, but there is no answer

DYNAMIC LEARNING

1

Dear student,

the *dynamic verb* is adjectival,
as expression, which is ironic

because errant, pedantically speaking,
but also oxymoronic

in being applied correctly to
a word, which is a verb,

and is dynamic in what it alludes to,
yet not in the meaningful way intended,

which isn't, though it is here now,
paradoxically.

Dear student, that is today's
dynamic lesson.

2

Dear student,

about this expression:
'The (abstract) nouns *two days*' –

no, this is as concrete as time gets,
calculated as precisely as this [though not by minutes
and seconds, I concede],

and their love has not been gulped by a 'dynamic verb'
but by water
that is literal and then metaphoric

and never – never – resolved by the
twee joining/unison/touch of wings
because actual love is not ever this finessed by feathers.

3

Dear student,

in the future
you must get your tenses right

as *tense verb*
is an inversion of something

learned in the past
but forgotten in the present.

And does 'had'
need this classification?

When they *had* that love,
then it was tense with anticipation.

4

Dearest student,

or not as much as what he loves her
is the most honest expression you

have shared
like what they did not, or her to him,

which you called ironic
and I, being older, would call despair,

dear young, earnest, learning student:

[asyndetic list].

ICT TEACHERS

ICT teachers who
suspect god is an AppleMac / junk poetry as spam if it doesn't reveal an IPS / are saving pen and paper for the apocalypse / personify their screamsavers / accept a computer will never be a proper noun / disconnect / dream of heliotrope keyboards in the sky / know haiku is a broadband sonnet form / WiFied their hi fi ages ago / never wear protection for a surge / surf their thinking / know backing it up isn't just a proclivity / don't get fourteen lines can be formatted / still read books with their hands

MORE AND MORE[1]
(after Poe)

Once upon a midnight dreary, as I wadded through words, weak and weary,
Over many a dull and spurious volume of philistine's lore -
While I nodded, nearly napping, suddenly in my head came a tapping,
As of some imposed curriculum rapping its song at my metaphoric door.
"Tis some friggin' new initiative," I swore, "tapping at my battered door -
                Labelled More and More and More."

Ah distinctly I remember it was in the bleak December;
And each past initiative's ember wrought its ghost upon the mind's floor.
Eagerly I wished the morrow of next year would bring a power that would not borrow
Others' ideas to inflict an increase on my sorrow - sorrow for not being as before,
For the rare and radiant teaching with the swish of an angel's wings before
                Becoming shameless automatons evermore.

---

[1] This and others to follow from a Christmas sequence written annually for teaching colleagues

21ST JUNE

On this longest day of summer
when the adjective qualifies the
noun

I have had my own significant
length of time examining
a naming of parts

as students respond to two
unseen poems about
weather

and whether personification
is spotted before the
simile

like a light flashing its
desperate hope for
recognition.

They have – well trained –
and most get the gists too:
one negative,

the other not, so an
extra mark for *positive*, perhaps
even the wind

blowing it into *antithesis*
and a move up
the ladder

which is an assessment metaphor.
Do not think this a
quiet rage

or unquiet one either –
it is just one long hot day of
monosyllables

until the enjambment kicks in.
So many felt the chill,
the thief who

stole summer scaring them
with palpable fear,
then a summer so perfect

if only they could have
read it today
in sweltering school halls

sweating out names
to explain
just in case, just in case

feeling and sharing feeling
is not enough anymore,
the glistening of japonica

more about the verb
than how a camellia smells
of a different name

but is the same.

PRIOR KNOWLEDGE

Taking the red-eye to wherever dawn becomes. A sea nearshored by foliage gives us hope for a future, but only before it disappears. The socialism of this is in colour-shares and the permanence of black and grey, as if prominence is what it *really* is when lost in emptiness. Loosening up the fundamentals of knowledge. To refine a gradgrind's stone sculpture to the fluidity of oils and random brushstrokes. When angular bookends embrace spheres we are reading the possibilities. Art practice is not controlled by the virus, but austerity makes a means of production its own disease. That grain, which I have seen before, is for all of us to consume.

MODERN LANGUAGES TEACHERS

Modern Languages teachers who
understand *Santa* is a corruption / blame Babel on linguistic ignorance / attach gender to words without fear of labelling / can talk drivel in any language / know a sonnet is more than sound in its etymology / speak when spoken to [by a foreigner] / translate for obfuscation / hear meaning in a strange sound / question Chomsky's innate beliefs / think grammar should be known beyond grandmas / know *annus mirabilis* sounds ironic every year / can multi-task in a semantic field / use *fuck* as a noun, verb, adjective, adverb, pronoun; or interjection, with its participle sometimes used as a strong emphatic, and the verb to *fuck* used transitively or intransitively, or just for the fucking fun of it

NATIONAL CURRICULUM AT SEA LIFE
(for Karis)

Karis will be seven as Spring begins
and today she reads beautifully
of *aquaria* and *anemones*,
watery new words from a brochure
to bathe and prepare her
for hot summer SATs that test within
landlocked and fixed boundaries,
      unable to reward
'the *o* flying away from *didn't* is an apostrophe'
or to understand, as it's only October,
the other beauty of her error
when reading the 'astonishing angels'
from which everything at Sea Life can be seen.

Most noticeable *angles* are actually hard
      as she'll learn and tell
herself when discovering what might have been.

MATHS TEACHERS

Maths teachers who
use numbers for disguise / count on their fingers / dream of being
an iambic pentameter / slide rule down inclines / know accuracy
isn't always right / add then divide then multiply then halve
sheep to sleep / are fractions rather than fractious / are wrong /
calculate the wisdom of not measuring / know sonnets love their
number of lines / think algebra is awry / would love the orgasm
of geometry / appreciate zero's pervasive existence / understand
heliotrope is more than a number

AEOLIAN HARPING ON
(after Coleridge)

My pensive colleagues! thy weary heads reclined
Thus on thine arms, most soothing sweet it is
To imagine each sat beside a Cot, any Cot o'ergrown
With flowers, and no thoughts of a targeted hurdle
To leap, just musings on Innocence and Love
And watching of clouds, that late were richly alight
With their vocation, and mark the rising stars
Serenely brilliant (such should Teaching be)
Shine opposite! How exquisite the sense
Snatch'd from yon school-field! and the playground so hushed!
But the inner murmur of what we distantly perceive
Tells us of defiance.

                That performance-related Loot
Placed naked in the seducer's casement, hark!
How by the derisory political breeze caress'd,
Like some toy maid half yielding to her payer,
It pours such sickly-sweet upgrading, as must needs
Tempt to expose the wrong! So that now, its strings
Professionally swept, the long vocational notes
Over conscientious surges sing and rise,
Such a soft floating teacherly sound
As twilight planners and markers make, when they at eve
Voyage on gentle gales of honest lesson plans,
Where Melodies round eyelid-dropping hours,
For every child, like birds of Paradise,
Nor pause, nor perch, relying on one another's wings

O! the one Life within school and at home,
Which defies money's promotion and becomes all,
(A slight in £££££s, a £££££-like desire to slight),
Rhythm is in thought, and joyance everywhere -
Methinks, it should have been impossible
Not to love such a job as one filled;
Where the breeze is self-induced, and surrounding air
Is Music paying the preferment.

ANGEL

Although I have never seen him float
or had to tell him off for
spreading his wings in the corridors,
the boy with wide expectant eyes
who waits each day outside the staffroom
is obviously an angel.

What I fear is that he may have come
to show all of us the trauma of innocence.

The tough boys with their black hair and
street-wise ways are going to test
his fragility by just being there,
and even I have to laugh when he looks at me
as if I can support or have the time
to help him through the day.

CROOKS

Crooks, according to thousands and thousands of
students, is primarily punctual, rising in alarm
to a day dreamed through gold-framed specs but
tightened by the reality of batterings he has endured.
They dream too of his multitude of shoes for all
terrains - bar the one he has to tread - and wishful
readings of his mauled life take on a life of their own,
being young and hopeful and having futures.
We know different. Though they too know he is old,
we understand the vernacular of what truly possesses
age; want to ask what snippet of the day he can
seize from dirty secrets isolated on his special shelf,
urge carpe diem to define a moment for those who
read into his chapter the risk of satisfying the self.

PRIOR KNOWLEDGE ENCORE

The beautiful lack of symmetry in a mirror reflection, a development in colour and shapes and size – how knowing one makes the other knowledgeable in such a contrary, defiant further. Links will not always. Dissemination-collation is the act of throwing hues onto a surface and organising it all into white. That blood seeping through. In *drawing on previous learning* you can fill a bag full of clauses to make 'interesting' sentences, but only if they make some sense rather than poetry. A gravity of yellow. To access an evidence bank you will need to pay with blind faith and cash. If moving away from Art it is for the rush of a diatribe.

PE TEACHERS

PE teachers who
wear shorts for a seasonal thrill / run to find out where they are
/ know a javelin only floats as far as it is thrown / think poetry
could use an exercise plan / can roll down a hill and survive /
know hurdles have no place in education / understand Sports
Day is for thinkers too / show you their endgame / feel the pain of
winning / understand that a relay is a political act / throw words
too / can get by without lunchtime / think a sonnet is raced in
fourteen lanes / only get high on lactic acid

SAUSAGES

I buy Mantel's *Wolf Hall* from one of the two
charity shops I visit today looking for second-
hand books or vinyl, a tome so large it has to

displace the wholemeal loaf purchased a few
moments before – the butcher's bangers
secured in another compartment of the bag.

On both of those recycling reading shelves
was a single and pinched copy of John Steinbeck's
Of Mice and Men, this year's exam over, and there

will never be the need again to read for study so the
school, like each discarding student, can care less if
future generations know about George and Lennie,

how dreams are futile, loneliness, why it's the girls
objectified, if there's any meaning to *sausage curls*.

CREATIVITIES PASSPORT[2]

Make night chocolate
Explore inside a float
Re-tell a hill
Teach like a pirate
Roll down a candle
Go to the moon
Walk barefoot on a self-portrait
Choreograph a share with investors
Make an exhibition look like a library
Make something that is taller than sand
Taste-test a story
Visit an art gallery and stay
Walk through a place of debate
Perform a heart poem
Pick litter in your air powered rocket
Learn a French story wet in the rain
Go home with an insect
See the sun and taste chapattis
Eat the stars
Write a hieroglyphics diary for a week
Visit a bridge and test its strength
Make a river
Eat something like a character from a book
Perform in front of leaf rubbings
Make a sandwich about your favourite film
Design and make a large-scale model of worship

2 Found in the then Education Secretary Damien Hind's 'Activities Passport'

Write in a pond
Vote for a tree
Try yoga on a picnic
Experience a Victorian speech
Walk to the top of a piece of collage
Visit a small creature
Make something out of a wood puppet

LEARNING SUPPORT TEACHERS

Learning Support teachers who
still have special needs / work from within / advise advisers to
help themselves / know how to misbehave / have to see beyond
nothing / live euphemism / triumph in minutia / help themselves /
tell Rudolf his nose is a blessing / take sonnets any way they come
/ can spell *heliotrope* / fake big strides / speak a little French / earn
more than they are paid

A STUDENT IS SINGING
(quite a bit after Adrian Mitchell)

A student is singing
and nobody listening
but the student who is singing:

philistines grab the earth and shower it.
The school is on fire.
Politicians wet the earth and flower it.
The school is on fire.
The schools are on fire.
Fetch the governors; the governors are on fire.
We will have to hide in a hole.
We will burn like coal.
All the students are on fire.

And a student is singing
and nobody listening
but the student who is singing.

PATHETIC FALLACY

Deep into examining,
I've just had a break outside
hacking back two hedges and
overgrowing bamboo –
a quick correction in the heat
of this July afternoon.

Now returned, I'm marking
these last three of the day,
razor-sharp and tuned and
admiring the decisions
and precisions I see as the
clearest fine lines.

SCIENCE TEACHERS

Science teachers who
know hypothesis is the beginning of ignorance / spread sheets /
just guess / know Doppler isn't a reindeer / experiment without
metaphor / add plugins for the searching / are literally / double
up / hear Doppler before it arrives, just / symbolise their FFTs
/ understand the ratio of hatred's displacement of love / think
Physics is Maths with oomph / know a loving spoonful is less than
a test tube full / hear a sonnet when it leaves, louder

ALL DOOM AND LITTLE FREEDOM
(after Ted Hughes)

A school's dark term shrunk to verbal barks and the clank of a ruckus -

And who is listening?
A tangled web, tense for a clue to the few who touch.
A pale face lifted, no frills or trimming - fear
to tempt a first reading to a tremor.

Now we are going home in the pain there, stooping under the wreath
of someone's
                                      indelible breath -
a stark shiver in our blood, trying to unfold the blur,
challenging to kill words in that ilk.

'Doom!' we cry suddenly, 'Doom! Doom!'

The buffoon has leapt back like a con-artist gazing fazed at the workers
that point at him un-amazed.

TF&D TEACHERS

TF&D Teachers who
fuel their own workshop lights / make more clocks than Switzerland / blueprint their lives / teach that sprouts are a cultural culinary perversion / are appalled at the Santa/chimney design paradox / sand the grain the righteous way / can craft nirvana out of cardboard / know their assistant rules / overcook on purpose / compose the tangible / would time travel back to the wonders of Woodwork / are their own appliances / solder sonnets with quicksilver rhymes / season all of the festive moment

WHERE DO EX-STUDENTS GO?

They go off
to new homes where
bedrooms give comfort
and do not define;

they go off
to new streets where
spaces are seen
beyond their confines;

they go off
to new friends whose
love is the memory of
crossing a line;

they go off
to new jobs where
hope advances what
dreaming declines;

they go off
to new cities whose
days and nights
offer to shine;

they go off
to new levels when
climbing is work and
arrival reclines;

they go off
to new worlds where
planets are spun
to their design;

they go off
to new lessons with
teaching when life's
learning refines.

A BOLD COLD AUTUMN

This is the first time for me in fifty plus years – or
from whenever it matters kicked in – and also for
half a million added-on kids, when Autumn arrives
with a sinister criminality. Call it what you like:
pathetic fallacy, personification, simile, a lexeme
of the wildest over-preparedness – the season to
come will make oxymoron a contradiction of itself.
Noting the line break half way through this possible
sonnet, an American poet can take his perfection
and forget making an impact. English enjambment
rules the forward thrust of negativity, and seasonal
expectation is painted with the red grimace of falling
leaves, even when that metaphor has been sucked dry
by a taught language so keen to explain away surprise.

MUSIC AND DRAMA TEACHERS

Music and Drama teachers who
feel invisible / know the pure melody of dissonance / pontificate
in their performance / eat all the pies / know the only reality is
absurd / dress up / want to be a bull's pizzle / have fuzz and wah
wah dreams / gesture sonnets on their stage / feel forgotten /
make love in iambic pentameters / are the curriculum / know
Ofsted is Oedipal / forgive

MR FERGY
(after Phillip Larkin)

This was Mr Fergy's room. He stayed
The whole time he was a teacher, till
They retired him. Decorated walls – posters now splayed –
Stand like the poor largesse of a teacher's last will

And testament: windows look out to land
Still goal-posted; littered, Mr Fergy took
This view to be a great bird in one hand,
And in the other, words from any good poet's book.

Behind the class door are ghosts: work in students' bags;
The offering 'I know the answer sir' or an obvious lie;
A view of the far corner of the field and smoke from fags;
Then the echoes of those who would always try.

Toughing it out with teaching year after year to drown
The jabbering of ignorance egged on by
Those who, intending to build, only tore down,
His sufferance was to always ask why

He kept on plugging at the days and days,
Likewise the tugging down from this good job's yolk.
It was always more than for the summer holidays
And Christmases when his *Stocking Fillers* spoke.

But if he stood and watched the December wind
Tousling memories, listened to what its blowing said,
Telling himself this was all there really was, and grinned,
And shivered, without shaking off the dread

That how he lived measures his own nature,
And at his age having no more to show
Than a collection of red printed volumes should make him sure
He warranted no better than what such words bestow.

DEBBIE

The church is dark and dull
but all the pews are full
as I sit with friends from school
wrapped in our sharing spool.

She wrote poems whispers Mark
and he smiles *but they were dark*
as he offers what she got
from the lessons that I taught.

Yes she snarled and she sneered
and I'd no idea what she feared
so for her noises and her looks
I gave paper, pen and books.

But with goading and with guile
anger turned a fleeting smile
and in such a switch as this
are the moments I will miss.

WHERE DO EX-TEACHERS GO?

They go back
to weekends where rooms
ignite sunshine
to douse the rains;

they go back
to ink-days where reds
annotate pleasure
instead of give pain;

they go back
to bedtimes where dreams
roll from mountains
to explode in plains;

they go back
to books where words
caress flesh
before the brain;

they go back
to heads where thoughts
brought by UFOs
melt track and trains;

they go back
to families where children
stretch their elastic
beyond the strain;

they go back
to loved ones where kisses
compose new songs
instead of refrains.

UNDERSTOOD

these young people
understand the elderly
aware of their defiance
and the fragility of bone
how a skull was
once covered in thicker hair
and how vernacular
could be seen as singsong
or sassy or
the voice of stubbornness
and though they sift
through nouns and verbs and
enjambment
they also empathise
and never mention autumn
or other old allusions

CAESURA

It is clear. This is it.
This feature. This fashion.
Overly taught. Over-taught.
[That was echo and repetition and tautology and cleverclogsness.
Also it.]
But this is really it. This caesura.
Is it medial? Terminal!

ON MY FIRST JOB
(after Ben Jonson)

Farewell, thou school of my right hand, and joy;
My chagrin was too much hope that in this employ
Of thirty years I would make it to the full and final day,
But exacted by harsh fate, time calls now to have its say:
You can not go further; not now. So should I
Lament a leaving that others will surely envie?
To have eventually scap'd school's and Fergy's rage
And, if nothing else, the whitening beard of age?
Rest in redundancy's ease, and, ask'd, say here goes Fergy,
Michael Glenn, his final piece of school poetry.
For fuck's sake, hence-forth, all swearing be such
As the job he loves may never forget too much.

STUDENTS

the students who listen and learn the students who come to school from their dark and dangerous homes the students who never put their hands up to answer questions the students who always want to answer questions the students who almost always answer questions wrong the students who have died the students who you meet years later but cannot remember their names the students who never return the students who are creeps the students who use school as a place to lounge the students who use school as a place of refuge the students who are brighter than their teachers the students who dance inside their heads the students who will never know how to dance the students without parents of their own the students who spend all of their free time finding places to smoke and hide the students who can scowl like olympic champions the students who argue all of the time the students who argue inside their own heads the students who are expelled the students who excel the students playing parts in plays the students who are athletes the students who can only manage to crawl through the day the students who get in the way the students who always smile the students who seem to always cry the students who have no friends the students who cannot face school the students who go bald before their time the students who have families the students who forget to attend their exams the students who will never know how to spell the students who write unforgettable words the students leaning back on their chairs the students making films for the future the students who laugh for no reason the students who laugh when you punish them the students who think they are useless the students who think they are god's gift the students who get lost on school trips the students who find themselves on school trips the students who gossip all of the time the students who draw stunning pictures

the students who can be abstract the students who will never be
abstract the students who become teachers the students who enter
the staffroom in awe the students who are always swearing with
their eyes the students who always swear out loud the students who
will never grow up the students who mimic me the students who
ignore me the students who made love on my desk the students
who never bring me an apple the students who give me the first
christmas card of the year the students who bother to say thank
you the students whose parents never say thank you the students
who arrive late for lessons the students who will always arrive late
for life the students who control the playground the students who
always play football the students who love the school canteen the
students who meet the person they'll marry at school the students
who act big because they are small the students who are always
absent the students who are always on holiday abroad the students
who buy me presents the students who wave from passing cars
the students who pull faces from bus windows the students who
moon the students on the edge of adulthood the students hiding
inside a packed room the students on permanent detention the
students who harm themselves the students who fall in and out of
love the students who never know what they will return to at the
end of the day the students who make discoveries the students
who never learn to regret the students who live inside their shell
the students who were born in darkness the students plugged into
music the students on drugs the students who worship the students
playing games before they have to grow up the students who are
interchangeable the students like ghosts in the corridors

my students